Towards the Single Currency

THE INTERGOVERNMENTAL CONFERENCE OF THE EUROPEAN UNION 1996

Federal Trust Papers Number Two

THE FEDERAL TRUST

The Federal Trust was founded in 1945 to study the future of democratic unity between states and peoples. The principal focus of its work has been the European Union and the United Kingdom's role within it.

The Federal Trust conducts enquiries, promotes seminars and conferences and publishes on a wide range of contemporary issues. Its current work programme includes studies of the completion of the European single market and the development of the information society in Europe.

The Trust has also established a major European education programme for sixth forms, universities and young leaders. It is involved in several projects to enhance the European dimension in the curriculum.

The Federal Trust is the UK member of the Trans-European Policy Studies Association (TEPSA).

PUBLISHED BY THE FEDERAL TRUST
158 BUCKINGHAM PALACE ROAD
LONDON SW1W 9TR

© FEDERAL TRUST FOR EDUCATION AND RESEARCH
MAY 1995

ISBN 0 90157 352 3
ISSN 1357 3314

THE FEDERAL TRUST IS A REGISTERED CHARITY

PRODUCED BY PSI PUBLISHING, LONDON NW1 3SR

PRINTED IN GREAT BRITAIN

Federal Trust Round Table

The Federal Trust has established a Round Table to discuss in depth the issues raised by the 1996 Intergovernmental Conference of the European Union, to monitor the processes of its preparation, negotiation and ratification, and to assess its outcome. A series of *Federal Trust Papers* is being published: the first, *State of the Union*, appeared in February 1995. The Round Table is chaired by Lord Jenkins of Hillhead, President of the European Commission 1977-81; the rapporteur is John Pinder, Chairman of the Federal Trust; the secretary is Andrew Duff, Director of the Trust, to whom any written comments should be addressed.

Members of the Round Table serve in an independent capacity and do not represent their organisations. They do not necessarily concur with all the opinions expressed in this *Federal Trust Paper*, but they support its general thrust and welcome it as a contribution to the debate about the future of the Union.

The Federal Trust is an independent charity and, as such, holds no political view of its own.

The Round Table includes:

Uwe Kitzinger
Christopher Layton
John Leech
Lord Lester QC
Jean-Victor Louis
Sarah Ludford
Peter Luff
Peter Mandelson MP
David Marquand
Andrew Marr
David Martin MEP
Richard Mayne
David Millar
Gary Miller
Frances Morrell
Edward Mortimer
Simon Nuttall
Sir Michael Palliser
Robin Pedler
John Pinder
Roy Pryce
Giles Radice MP
Paul Richards
Keith Richardson
Francesco Rossolillo

Malcolm Rutherford
Derek Scott
Michael Shackleton
Eleanor Sharpston
Baron Snoy d'Oppuers
John Stevens MEP
Susan Strange
Alastair Sutton
Susie Symes
Dick Taverne QC
Christopher Taylor
Anthony Teasdale
Lord Tugendhat
Sandy Walkington
Helen Wallace
WilliamWallace
Graham Watson MEP
Wolfgang Wessels
Martin Westlake
Richard Whitman
Shirley Williams
John Williamson
Ernest Wistrich
Stephen Woodard

Glossary

CAP	Common Agricultural Policy
EC	European Community
ECB	European Central Bank
Ecofin	Council of Economic and Finance Ministers
Ecu	European Currency Unit
EMI	European Monetary Institute
EMU	Economic and Monetary Union
ERM	Exchange Rate Mechanism
ESCB	European System of Central Banks
EU	European Union
GDP	Gross Domestic Product
GNP	Gross National Product
IGC	Intergovernmental Conference
NAFTA	North American Free Trade Agreement

Foreword by Sir Roy Denman

Economic and Monetary Union (EMU) is the central feature of the Treaty on European Union, signed at Maastricht in February 1992. This was not a sudden whim of zealous federalists. It is a logical step following the creation first of a customs union and then a single market.

Towards the Single Currency is the second of several papers by a wide-ranging Round Table, brought together under the aegis of the Federal Trust, to explain the background to the fundamental choices which Britain will face in the Intergovernmental Conference of 1996 on the future of the European Union. The first paper, *State of the Union*, published in February 1995, dealt with the strategic issues involved in deepening the unification of Europe. This paper looks at what is involved for Britain in EMU.

It was the chairman of our Round Table, Lord Jenkins, who as President of the European Commission, took the bold initiative which led to the establishment in 1979 of the highly structured Exchange Rate Mechanism which the UK was late in joining and early to leave. It was left to the Treaty of Maastricht to establish the project in detail and to commit member states in practice to its accomplishment.

The Treaty lays down a detailed timetable for member states to fulfil various criteria for economic and monetary convergence. It is possible that at the European Council at Dublin in December 1996 some member states might decide to go forward in 1997. It is more likely that this will happen in 1999. The UK has so far opted out. Should it then join them?

There are powerful arguments for doing so. The elimination of exchange rate fluctuations would cut transaction costs and reduce the expense and fuss for the ordinary traveller. It would also stimulate investment and increase employment. Staying out would not only lose these advantages but would expose the pound, on its own, to damaging speculation. Britain's influence would be marginalised in an increasingly integrated European Union.

The doubts centre on three issues. Is EMU likely to work? Will it involve an unacceptable loss of sovereignty? Will it mean a straitjacket of disinflation and high unemployment?

We do not find any of these doubts compelling.

Since the Second World War Britain has constantly misjudged the momentum of the move towards unity in Continental Europe. We have followed a path of high inflation and steady devaluation. The economic record of our partners has been markedly better. They have the political will to make a single currency succeed. If we remain outside we shall not only forfeit the advantage of lower costs and lasting economic stability but become an offshore irrelevance. If we delay joining we shall find, as we have before, that the rules are written without us.

The United Kingdom should take the decision to join a single currency as soon as practicable and in the meantime prepare for it by improving the competitiveness of its economy and by participating fully in negotiations over the shape of economic and monetary union.

Roy Denman

May 1995

Britain and EMU

What approach should Britain take to Monetary Union? While it is unlikely that the forthcoming Intergovernmental Conference (IGC) will make any attempt to amend the programme laid down by the Maastricht Treaty, Economic and Monetary Union is still likely to exercise a powerful influence on the discussions. In any event, the third stage of EMU casts a large shadow forward and Britain cannot indefinitely postpone decisions about what its stance should be.

EMU was not invented at Maastricht. It was officially declared to be the goal of the European Community as early as 1969. Nor is it, as some have supposed, solely concerned with monetary policy and convergence criteria to ensure that monetary policy can be effective. The Treaty itself regards EMU as essential to the aim of a balanced development of economic activities, which include a high level of employment and the raising of standards of living and the quality of life.

The fundamental aim of EMU is to remove for all time exchange rate uncertainties between EMU members to their mutual advantage. These prevent the full benefits of the single market from being realised: where businesses have had to deal with currency fluctuations between European currencies of over 20%, investment has been prejudiced and jobs have suffered. Even large companies are disadvantaged by currency fluctuations, but small companies, on whom future job creation largely depends, suffer most of all, and they are also more affected by the costs of foreign exchange transactions.

The instability of currencies has been aggravated by the increasing flows of funds across exchanges and the relative insignificance of national currency reserves. Attempts to moderate these flows exact a heavy price in premium rates of interest. EMU would protect its members from speculative raids.

At the same time Europe's own capital markets are still fragmented by the restrictive rules in force in some states which inhibit investment abroad. EMU would eliminate these restrictions and would speed the creation of probably the largest and most liquid capital market in the world. This would go to fund the expansion of Europe's infrastructure which promises to make a vital contribution to investment, growth and competitiveness.

Some oppose EMU because they are concerned that the European Central Bank (ECB) will be unaccountable to the public and will lack public support. While there are detailed requirements for the ECB to report to governments and to the European Parliament, we agree that there should be wider consultation, transparency and parliamentary scrutiny than the Maastricht Treaty provides.

Devaluation and unemployment

The convergence required by the Maastricht Treaty may not be achieved by 1997, but transition to the final stage is extremely likely in 1999 — especially in the light of the economic recovery now taking place throughout Europe. Questions remain about how far EMU is desirable or feasible.

Are national economic differences too great to make it dangerous to remove the safety valve of devaluation? The arguments about devaluation go to the root of the merits of EMU. Critics refer to the likelihood of outside shocks affecting states differently and point to the unhappy experience of German unification and the weaknesses of the Exchange Rate Mechanism (ERM) as arguments that the right to devalue must be kept.

However, the history of devaluations generally shows their advantages to be short-lived. Historically this has been true in Britain's case. Although our recent devaluation on leaving the ERM has so far been successful, the circumstances were exceptional, because there was enough slack in capacity to absorb both a rise in exports and a limited rise in demand. No one can be sure that this present advantage will be retained. Indeed the best way of safeguarding it would be to enter a monetary union at a time when, as now, we are competitive. More generally, the experience of the ERM is a poor guide to what would happen in EMU, mainly because the ERM invites currency speculation, whereas EMU, once established, rules it out.

Nor is the experience of German unification relevant to the case for EMU. There was no prior convergence of any kind between East and West Germany. Further, unification in one country — and in Berlin, even one city — is bound to lead to wage harmonisation. In a monetary union between separate states the pressures for wage parity will be much weaker.

Will EMU mean centralised economic decision-taking, leading to a superstate? We think not. There are possible advantages in centrally organised transfers between states to help with the convergence of the poorer states or to help states in temporary difficulties. At present transfer payments amount to only 1.25% of EU GDP, which offers little scope for equalisation. But it is quite clear that there is strong opposition from the major donors to an increase in fiscal transfers; and even if there were no opposition, it is likely that Maastricht's budgetary disciplines would rule them out. Structural problems of unemployment will remain, as they have been since the founding of the Union, a matter for the governments of the member states.

Should Britain join?

There is no point in Britain simply hoping that EMU will not happen. Nor are we likely to maximise our influence in current and future discussions by arguing that EMU should be postponed. A core of countries is committed to going ahead. Our record is one of joining everything late. If we were once again to argue that the time was not right, our contentions would be dismissed out of hand.

Our conclusion is that Britain has much to gain from joining EMU and much to lose from staying out. Over the past 25 years, our inflation has been more than twice as high as Germany's. Monetary management by an independent ECB modelled on the Bundesbank, in a union which only countries with a record of sustainable low inflation can join, holds out a far better prospect for lower inflation and lower interest rates. Staying out means having to defend the pound with premium interest rates against constant speculation that we shall once again be forced to devalue.

Lower interest rates will be good for investment and therefore for jobs. They will be good for those who have to pay off their mortgages. By contrast, staying out will place our industry at a disadvantage because our companies will continue to bear the burdens of transaction costs and exchange rate uncertainties from which our competitors are freed. This will make us less competitive in EU and worldwide markets. Foreign investment is also likely to be lower, with further adverse effect on jobs.

Lastly, there is a real danger that turning our backs on the goal which other member states have accepted will lead to a more fundamental parting of the ways. A deep divide could open between ourselves and EMU members. Relations could easily deteriorate. We could find ourselves in a one-way street out of the European Union altogether.

Towards the Single Currency [1]

In our first Paper, *State of the Union*, we laid out the strategic argument for deepening the unification of Europe.[2] In this Paper we examine Economic and Monetary Union; we consider the important economic and monetary arguments and their political implications; we discuss, in the light of experience since Maastricht, whether EMU will prove to be practicable; and we set out the options for Britain.

Background

Economic and Monetary Union is the central feature of the Treaty on European Union, signed at Maastricht in February 1992. The Treaty contains a carefully prepared plan to integrate the monetary policies of the member states with the overriding aim of achieving price stability. This is intended not simply, or even mainly, for the sake of European political unification but in order to achieve the economic purposes of the European Union, whose main goal is to 'promote economic and social progress which is balanced and sustainable'.[3] EMU, therefore, is not a conspiracy of unbridled Europeanism or monetarism: indeed, together with the common market, it is deemed to be the indispensable basis for an economic policy whose specific aims are:

'a harmonious and balanced development of economic activities, sustainable and non-inflationary growth respecting the environment, a high degree of convergence of economic performance, a high level of employment and of social protection, the raising of the standard of living and quality of life, and economic and social cohesion and solidarity among Member States'.[4]

Nor was the EMU project a sudden invention of Maastricht. Once the customs union had been achieved by the then six member states of the European Economic Community in 1968, ways began to be explored of consolidating the integration process. In 1969 the summit meeting at The Hague declared the goal of EMU, and set up a high-level group under the Luxembourg prime minister, Pierre Werner, to produce recommendations. The Werner Report advocated a gradual narrowing of exchange rate fluctuations leading to an irrevocable fixing of currencies.[5] This approach was adopted by the Council, but the other half of Werner's proposals — for strong centralised decision-making and the harmonisation of budgetary and fiscal policies — was not. Unsurprisingly, the experiment was quickly blown off course by the international dollar crisis. A European Monetary Cooperation Fund proved too weak to sustain the EC 'snake' (with fluctuations of 2.25%) inside the international 'tunnel' (4.5% fluctuation against the dollar).[6]

At the same time, the accession of the UK, Denmark and Ireland and the growing diversity of the Community made it more likely that a multi-speed approach to monetary union would emerge. Another study of the future of the Community, the Tindemans Report, emphasised that while all member states would be bound by the objective of EMU, some could — and therefore should — proceed faster than others.[7]

Roy Jenkins, as President of the Commission, launched the idea of monetary union again in 1977. This led to the establishment of the European Monetary System in 1979, with its highly structured Exchange Rate Mechanism centred on the European Currency Unit (Ecu), keeping the currencies of the participating states within 2.25% of their central rates, which were to be altered only by unanimous agreement among the participants. The multi-speed reality of European integration was exemplified when the UK declined to put sterling within the ERM. The Single European Act (1986) gave a legal base to the European Monetary System and incorporated the goal of EMU as a Treaty objective. But it was left to the Treaty of Maastricht to establish the project in detail and to commit member states in practice to its accomplishment.

EMU and the Treaty of Maastricht

Economic and Monetary Union as defined by Maastricht is primarily concerned with achieving price stability as the basis for economic and social progress.[8] Its goal is to eliminate exchange rate instability by requiring the irrevocable locking together of exchange rates and the creation of a single monetary policy independently pursued by a European System of Central Banks. This stage is to be followed rapidly by the introduction of a single currency to replace those national currencies locked together.

EMU imposes strict rules about government deficits. There is to be no printing of money to cover them, and the EU may not bail out member states with non-manageable debts. On the advice of the Commission, the Council may lay down specific measures to correct an excessive government deficit, and publish them, so influencing the government's borrowing powers in the markets. If a member state chooses to disregard the Council's remedial measures, sanctions may be imposed against the offending government by a qualified majority vote of the Council excluding the vote of the government in question. The Council may also require specific information to be published before the government issues bonds or securities, invite the EIB to reconsider its lending policy towards the member state concerned, or require the government to make a non-interest bearing deposit with the ECB until the excessive deficit is corrected.[9] All these provisions taken together mean that laxity in public finance is severely discouraged. In theory, at least, it should be possible for the government of a member state in a domestic crisis to go bust.

The Maastricht Treaty lays down a detailed timetable for member states to fulfil various criteria for economic and monetary convergence so that they may pass to the third phase of EMU in preparation for the introduction of the single currency. We are already in Stage Two, which began on 1 January 1994. The earliest decision about Stage Three will be taken at the European

Council in Dublin as early as December 1996, when after receiving reports by the Commission and the European Monetary Institute (the embryonic European Central Bank), the heads of government will assess which states could go forward. If a technical majority of member states so exists, and progress has been made on preparing the institutions (including making the Bank of England independent if the UK opts in), the European Council will then decide, by a qualified majority, whether it is appropriate to go forward and, if so, to set the date. The question of the size of the technical majority is complicated by derogations for Britain and Denmark from the transition to Stage Three: it is probable that the quorum will be defined as seven out of thirteen member states, rather than eight out of fifteen.

If, as looks likely, one or all of these preconditions are not met in 1997, the Treaty provides that Stage Three will begin on 1 January 1999 with as many (or as few) member states moving irreversibly to a single currency as then fulfil the convergence criteria. But the German Bundestag has resolved that it will approve — or not — any recommendation that the conditions have been met before accepting German participation in Stage Three. Only a veto by the German parliament or constitutional court could then effectively halt EMU. Such a block is improbable, as both Helmut Kohl and his likely successors are all strongly committed to European unification, and there is no evidence to suggest that in the elections to the Bundestag that must take place in October 1998 this strategy will be over-turned.[10]

Advantages of one currency: stability, investment, costs

It is striking that, despite the uncertainties that still surround EMU, the governments of all the member states, including at least initially the UK, appear to have concluded that the case for staying on the course set at Maastricht is strong. Governments have repeatedly affirmed their intention to make EMU succeed. At Copenhagen in June 1993 the European Council acknowledged the interdependence between the completion of the single market, the importance of a high level of capital investment and the need to stabilise the international monetary system. They endorsed the outline of a programme for economic recovery presented by Commission President Jacques Delors, in which the guidelines asserted that a single currency would:

- consolidate the single market and create the necessary conditions for fair and productive competition;

- make investment more attractive, both in the Community and outside, and generally stimulate savings to provide the necessary funds for major infrastructure projects;[11]

- have a stabilising effect on the international monetary system and preempt the speculation responsible for so much instability and uncertainty.

At the heart of the case for a single currency lies the need for greater stability of the European currencies. Like the North American Free Trade Agreement (NAFTA), where monetary union was not discussed, but unlike the USA itself, the European Union's large single market exists at present with separate national currencies, most of which are loosely connected inside the ERM within margins of 15%. The famous 'level playing field' established by the EU for the free movement of capital (and goods, services and people) applies to freedom from exchange control, not to the ironing out of exchange rate fluctuations. As Eddie George, the Governor of the Bank of England, has pointed out in a recent lecture:

'If we ask why we should be contemplating a move to monetary union, the economic — as distinct from the possible political — answer would have to be that the permanent elimination of exchange rate fluctuations between the member states would promote economic prosperity within Europe by increasing further the benefits to be derived from the single European market'.[12]

Uncertainty inhibits investment. In the early years of the single market, uncertainty about exchange rate fluctuations has proved to be a severe restraint on the investment decisions of manufacturing businesses. Even in low to medium-tech industries it takes about five years to bring a new plant on stream. Looking back over the past five years, business has had to cope with variations of 20% or more between European currencies. The effect of these fluctuations is even more dramatic because they occur not progressively but suddenly, making a nonsense of pricing policy in the internal market.

Countries which have suffered particularly from speculative attacks on their currencies, and which have had to take measures to protect them, will almost certainly benefit from lower interest rates. The combination of lower rates and the removal of uncertainty will have a positive and cumulative effect on manufacturing confidence and investment. This seems to be the view of a big majority of British industrialists.[13]

Moreover, a single currency will save costs. Although banks will lose profit from their intra-European currency conversion, for the consumer the single currency will cut out the costs and exchange rate risks (and the fuss) of changing currencies across the internal borders of the European Union. It would help to make a reality of the freedom of movement of ordinary people. Big companies can generally keep transaction costs low and cope with short-term currency risk. But for smaller companies the elimination of currency costs and risks are of substantial significance. Small and medium-sized enterprises have to pay a bigger share of their profits for currency transactions: many of them, for that reason, are postponing entering the European single market altogether.[14] As the small and medium-sized business sector is the most likely generator of new jobs, the removal of the currency differential would be an important factor in greater employment opportunities as well as future economic growth.

Capital market integration: why a single market needs a single currency

The creation of the European single market in 1993 and the Treaty of Maastricht, together with the globalisation of financial markets, has effectively liberalised all capital movements throughout the Union.[15] This has introduced an element of instability that proved incompatible with the regime of semi-fixed exchange rates of the ERM. On 'Black Wednesday' in September 1992, Britain's foreign exchange reserves were decimated as the equivalent of 5% of the country's pension and life assurance assets were hedged against sterling's depreciation. Although foreign exchange reserves held by national central banks are considerably higher than they were twenty years ago, they are falling relative to the stock of financial assets within the EU. As funded pension schemes outgrow state schemes and the stock of private assets continues to rise, the foreign exchange reserves of the member states will appear diminutive. Instability in foreign exchange and capital markets in Europe (and elsewhere) is likely to continue to force national governments to pay high risk premiums on interest rates in an attempt to moderate capital movements. Monetary policy has a choice of way forward: either member states find themselves forced to devalue their currencies thereby creating tensions within the single market that could in time lead to disintegration; or they enjoy sustained convergence between their economies, like Germany and Benelux where the mark, franc and guilder enjoy a stable relationship. The latter is the route of the Maastricht Treaty.

The USA is able to take advantage of a monetary union because of its high mobility of labour and capital. In the European Union, it is the scale of cross-border investment which matters most. As Delors indicated in his 1993 White Paper *Growth, Competitiveness, Employment: the challenges and ways forward into the 21st century*, a single currency would make investment more attractive and would generally stimulate savings to provide the necessary funds for major infrastructure projects such as those providing the framework for the information society.[16]

Freedom of capital movement is a cornerstone of the single market. However, despite the success of the Capital Movements Directive, the prime agents of freer capital movement, in particular Europe's pension funds, are still highly fragmented, both in structure and in investment orientation. The Commission sought but failed to get agreement to the Pension Fund Directive, introducing freedom of cross-border membership, freedom to provide the service of managing pension funds and freedom of cross-border investment of fund assets. The biggest obstacle to the liberalisation of occupational pension schemes was the desire by national governments to retain savings in their own capital markets with a view to funding their own deficits. At present just two member states, the UK and the Netherlands, account for nearly nine-tenths of all private pension funds in the EU. But the pressure for reform is growing as public pensions schemes are stretched to breaking point by Europe's increasingly ageing population. By the end of the decade, the size of assets under institutional management is likely to double. Indeed, were financial institutions throughout the EU to grow as large in relation to GNP as they are in the UK, assets under management would quadruple to some Ecu 6000 billion at current prices.[17]

The advent of monetary union, and particularly a single currency, will remove the remaining obstacles to greater capital mobility in Europe. A more uniform pricing of risk in the EU would improve the efficiency with which capital is allocated. Indeed the EU could become the largest and most liquid capital market in the world, acting as a powerful magnet to investors from the USA and Japan. At the same time greater liquidity would raise financial asset prices, thereby reducing the cost of capital and leading to more risk-bearing equity being available to European industry.[18] Moreover, the advent of monetary union would make it easier for member states and their regions to borrow in an integrated European bond market. A major difference between

European EMU and some federal systems will be in the smaller scale of grant-aid finance from the EC budget to the peripheral or poorer regions via the cohesion and structural funds. But the extension of finance from public-private partnerships towards the building of Trans-European networks could become very significant indeed. In the US, public-private partnerships have been highly effective in regenerating declining cities and regions.

The consequences of failure

Not only would a single currency bring certain positive advantages, but it should also be borne in mind that failure to achieve the Maastricht objectives entails serious dangers for the single market and for the European Union itself. Economic and monetary union was by far the most ambitious objective of Maastricht. All EU governments, except Britain and Denmark, have bound themselves by Treaty to the aim of EMU. If the objective now were to be abandoned or postponed indefinitely, contrary to the Treaty's terms, it would be the most serious failure since the founding of the Community. A return to devaluations of EU currencies would weaken the single market more than if the goal of EMU had never been declared. Protectionism could resurface. The setback to the process of closer political union could also prove divisive to an extent that would greatly damage the European Union itself.

The prospects for Stage Three

In a formal sense, the question of EMU, and of how member states are to reach it, was settled at Maastricht. Nevertheless, although the Intergovernmental Conference of 1996 need not revisit the economic part of the Treaty it cannot realistically ignore it. For one thing, many detailed and technical decisions still have to be taken — about the working of the European Central Bank, the European System of Central Banks and the Council of economic and finance ministers, about democratic accountability, and, last but not least, about the design, production and introduction of the single currency.

Undue difficulty in dealing with these could affect adversely the atmosphere at the IGC. In particular, French readiness to concede to Germany's proposals for strengthening the European Parliament is likely to depend on German willingness to resolve the outstanding problems of EMU in a way that will enable Stage Three to start in 1999 at the latest.

To assess the capability of states to make the transition to Stage Three, the Maastricht Treaty set down five criteria concerning inflation, long-term interest rates, exchange rates and government deficits and debt. In TABLE ONE we set out how those criteria are currently being met by the fifteen member states.

The recent recession has made the inflation criterion relatively easy to meet for a majority of countries, at least for the time being. Convergence is to be defined as an annual rate of increase of consumer price indices not more than 1.5% above the average of the three best performing states in the previous year. Twelve out of the fifteen states, including the UK, are at present forecast to meet this criterion in 1996.[19]

Under the Treaty, long-term rates must not exceed by over 2% the average of those of the three best performing states in terms of price stability. Twelve states are forecast to achieve this in 1996, although long-term interest rates will have converged by moving upwards instead of down.

The exchange rate criterion, that a currency will have remained for at least two years within the 'normal fluctuation margins', was drafted on the assumption that the ERM would continue to observe its original margins of 2.25%.[20] Following the August 1993 currency crisis, however, the band has been widened to 15% on either side. The European Council could interpret the Treaty criterion as meaning that a currency must be within a reasonably stable relationship with its peers for two years before a decision is made about Stage Three, although it is far from certain that Germany, for one, would accept less rigour than was originally envisaged.

The EMU Convergence Criteria

Percentage change

	Consumer price deflator change 1996	Government long bond interest rate 1996	General government deficit/GDP 1996	Gross government debt/GDP 1996	Government debt ratio trend 1994-96
Austria	3.1	7.5	4.2	61	rising
Belgium	2.6	8.0	4.0	136	falling
Denmark	2.4	8.7	2.2	78	stable
Finland	2.7	8.7	2.5	86	rising
France	2.1	7.5	3.9	56	rising
Germany	2.4	7.3	2.0	59	stable
Greece	9.0	17.5	12.9	128	rising
Ireland	2.7	8.5	1.5	79	falling
Italy	3.5	11.7	7.9	129	rising
Luxembourg	2.7	7.5	+2.0	10	stable
Netherlands	2.5	7.3	2.7	78	stable
Portugal	4.4	8.5	4.8	72	rising
Spain	4.4	8.8	4.7	66	rising
Sweden	3.1	10.8	7.3	111	rising
UK	3.3	8.1	2.1	49	stable
EC 12	3.1	8.4	3.9	73	
Three best	2.3	7.8			
Limit	3.8	9.8	3.0	60	

Sources: European Commission *1995 Annual Economic Report*; OECD *Economic Outlook*, December 1994; UK *Financial Statement and Budget Report 1995-96*.

The main constraint of the Treaty is that in Stage Three 'member states shall avoid excessive government deficits'.[21] The criteria set are that deficits should not be more than 3% of GDP and that the general government gross debt should not be more than 60% of GDP. Deficits can exceed 3% only if they have 'declined substantially and continuously and reached a level that comes close to the reference value' or, alternatively, the excess is 'only exceptional and temporary'. The debt/GDP ratio can exceed

60% only if the ratio is 'sufficiently diminishing and approaching the reference value at a satisfactory pace'.[22] The 3% deficit to GDP and the 60% debt to GDP ratios are the 'reference values'.[23] Of the two, the actual size of the deficit is the more important. The Treaty requires other factors to be taken into account by the Commission in deciding whether to invoke the excessive deficit procedure, including a budgetary review of the member state concerned.

Any interpretation of the fiscal provisions of EMU depends on a political judgement about how the Commission and the Council will choose to apply the Maastricht criteria. As things stand, only Germany, Luxembourg and the UK are forecast to fulfil both the deficit and debt criteria by 1996; in eight member states debt/GDP ratios will probably be rising. Given Europe's current economic recovery, however, the position is likely to be transformed by 1999.

Problems and uncertainties

Many difficult choices about EMU remain to be settled. In essence, what has been agreed in the Treaty is a framework for the conduct of monetary policy. Much attention will, quite properly, focus on how in Stage Two the European Monetary Institute (EMI) proposes to make this new framework operational, in itself no small task. Effective management of the European economy will, however, require accommodations to be reached on a much wider range of policy areas, and it is clear that many of these have been inadequately prepared.

Nobody pretends that monetary union will work without economic convergence between member states. Convergence, however, is not the same as union — and a failure to make that distinction has confused the debate. In one sense the term 'economic and monetary union' is misleading: a complete economic union would exist were all the levers of economic policy to be centralised — in other words, not only monetary policy but fiscal and other economic policies also. This is not what is proposed for the European Union. The EMU of Maastricht does not mean a single EU economy run by a single government with a single budget and single taxation. There will still be national debate on priorities for taxing and spending, provided that the limits set for deficits are respected. The member states are, however, to regard their economic policies as a 'matter of common concern' and to seek to coordinate them in Ecofin — the Council of economic and finance ministers.[24] There will be a single monetary policy, and the exchange rate policy of the Ecu will be set by the European Central Bank within the framework of any exchange rate system for the Ecu in relation to other currencies that may be determined by the Council.

Monetary union, as we have seen, will transfer responsibility for monetary policy from the member state level to the European Central Bank, acting together with national central banks in the European System of Central Banks (ESCB). Yet although there is a clear remit to pursue price stability, what this will mean in practice has not been specified. How tight monetary policy is to be will depend on whether an inflation target is actually set, and if so how low, as well as on other factors, such as fiscal policy. A key question is how the convergence criteria will be interpreted once Stage Three has been reached. The devil is really in the detail: for example, is 3% of GDP to be regarded as the ceiling for government deficits or as an average over the economic cycle?

Equally uncertain is how far problems will arise from the division of responsibility for monetary and fiscal policy, with monetary policy decided at Union level and fiscal policy by the member states (within the deficit limits). Germany in the early 1990s illustrated the difficulties that can arise when monetary and fiscal policies are at odds. The aftermath of German unification was an exceptional case. But there will be problems in achieving a collective European fiscal stance that is both compatible with monetary policy and appropriate for European macroeconomic circumstances.

There is, then, a policy paradox at the heart of the Maastricht Treaty. It removes, over a period, national freedom of decision in monetary policy. This means that national governments may need to make greater use of fiscal policy in order to achieve their objectives for output and employment. However, governments will also be constrained by their Treaty obligation towards achieving stable prices and sound public finance. In practice, therefore, their freedom of manoeuvre in fiscal policy will be limited. The governments, in fact, have bound themselves to be disciplined, and the ultimate condition of EMU is that they prove themselves trustworthy in this regard — and that their electorates grow to accept such discipline too.

Although there is no necessary link between monetary union and other spheres of economic policy, the highest tier of government in a union typically assumes responsibility for considerably more than macroeconomic policy. This is partly because there are efficiency arguments for involving the higher tier, as is recognised in the articulation of the principle of subsidiarity. Equity arguments are, however, also relevant, especially if the balance of costs and benefits of union differs between participants. In this regard, the role of the higher tier is to mediate between net winners and net losers.

In the current political context, a further transfer of power from member states to the European level is highly unlikely even if it were desirable. The US example is not, therefore, directly relevant. But it is worthwhile to ask just how far the Union is or may be drawn into the general management of fiscal policy or in areas such as structural policies, regulation, jobs, welfare and redistribution policies. It is after all, part of the case made against a single currency that it will inevitably lead to a strong central government, on the grounds that you cannot centrally determine monetary policy without taking power to determine economic policy centrally as well.

In the EU at present, there are various common structural policies, including the CAP and pan-European research initiatives. The activities of the structural funds, in so far as their stated purpose is to improve the competitiveness of regions which receive support, also aim to advance structural objectives. In the same vein, support for trans-European networks is seen as a means of improving the efficiency of the European supply side. The scale of the transfers forms as much as 6 - 7% of the GDP of Ireland and Portugal — and is evidence of a significant political solidarity between member states.

EU involvement in regulatory policies is substantial in key areas such as competition policy, external trade policy, health and safety and certain other aspects of labour regulation. The main thrust of the single market has been to establish a common regulatory framework and many of the measures advocated in the recent White Paper on social policy would extend the regulatory influence of the institutions of the Union.[25] By contrast, the supranational tier currently has little or no say in job and welfare policies. The structural funds have some impact on training, but the scale of these operations is limited. On welfare and redistribution, the role of the European tier is limited to a Council Recommendation on the objectives of social protection.

It could be argued that the absence of the supranational tier from these social areas will become increasingly untenable as union is consolidated. A key argument is that EMU itself affects the welfare of participants (both relatively and absolutely). This raises the issue, to which we return below, of the need for compensatory fiscal flows similar to those that played such a crucial role in the recent German monetary union. To put it a different way, the choices that are made in these areas will signal what kind of union the EU is to become. At the moment, fiscal transfers are justified mainly for structural ends rather than for stabilisation or redistributive purposes. No substantive change is proposed under the terms of Stage Three of Maastricht.

At present the EC budget amounts to only 1.25% of EU GDP: to increase it to a size that would allow for very much larger fiscal transfers between low unemployment and high unemployment regions postulates a sort of United States of Europe that nobody seems to want.[26] The route chosen by Maastricht, on the other hand, imposes major constraints on public spending, including, by inference, on that of the Union itself. Under EMU all states are obliged to undertake structural modernisation of their economies, involving competition, liberalisation, education and training, in the expectation that, in time, the poorer states could achieve a level of economic performance comparable to that of the Union's richest members. The lack of such structural reform would have the effect of dividing the Union between a rich federal core and a poorer outer tier. Such a prospect is particularly alarming to the governments of Spain, Portugal, Italy and Greece, but it also holds out a clear warning for the countries of Central Europe that are seeking membership.

The fact is that a significant increase in fiscal transfers between either existing or future member states of the Union is unlikely to occur both because of the political opposition of the richer states to paying for it and because of the budgetary discipline imposed on them by Maastricht. Moreover, substantial fiscal transfers *between* member states are unlikely to be necessary if member states are properly convergent: fiscal transfers *within* member states will remain more important.

How the fiscal policy of the Union develops in practice will be largely the responsibility of the Council (Ecofin), who are charged, as we have seen, to monitor the economic performance of member states and to take action against those that incur 'excessive government deficits'. The financial markets will watch very closely the development of Ecofin and will be much influenced by how tough the Council is prepared to be with errant governments. Ecofin will become a powerful formation of the Council, and take on much of the character of an economic policy-making cabinet.

The 'real' economy

Some have suggested that the forthcoming IGC should broaden the convergence criteria of Maastricht to include indicators of 'real' economic performance, such as long-term trends in employment, regional balance, and growth. We find, however, that few governments are remotely interested in disturbing the Maastricht package; and some, notably the Germans, are strongly opposed. It should be remembered that economic and social progress already constitutes a central objective of the European Union, and, enshrined as it is in the Treaty, informs the whole context within which the project of EMU is being developed. The ECB will have always to take into account the general economic objectives of the Treaty. In our view, therefore, to try to get the forthcoming IGC to supplement the Maastricht convergence criteria with new ones stipulating broad conditions about rising living standards would be largely a cosmetic exercise. In any case, the obvious risk of opening Pandora's box means that such an attempt will surely be resisted by the majority of member states.

Clearly, however, real economic indicators do matter to the success or otherwise of EMU: if they were expected to be negative for most or all member states, the intellectual case for EMU would be very weak, and its political prospects negligible; if the impact on the indicators is expected to be negative in any one state, its reluctance to join the EMU would be understandable. What is important, after all, is not EMU for its own sake but the pursuit of prudent monetary and fiscal policies; if we could always guarantee monetary and fiscal policies of such prudence as to make permanently fixed exchange rates a natural and credible outcome, a formal EMU project would hardly be necessary; if we are condemned always to have imprudent monetary and fiscal policies, EMU will not work. The convincing argument for EMU, therefore, lies in the proposition that its whole effect in terms of the added value of European integration in building a competitive social market economy and in increasing investment will benefit all, at least over the longer term.

Nevertheless, unemployment remains one of the principal concerns of those who are opposed or doubtful about EMU. This leads us to consider the argument that in the present state of divergence between the real economies of the EU it would be dangerous to link currencies and jettison the safeguard of devaluation.

Problems of EMU: losing the right to devalue

The Governor of the Bank of England has put the nub of the case both for and against EMU. Eddie George agrees that 'sustained monetary and exchange rate stability within the European Union is wholly desirable and would substantially increase the benefits of the single market by improving the efficiency of resource allocation within Europe'.[27] He adds that the 'economic argument for monetary union is that it would deliver greater union-wide stability in practice, and, importantly, that it would carry greater conviction with investors that intra-European stability would be maintained into the medium and long term'. His worry, however, is that 'given that monetary union removes the 'safety valve' of exchange rate realignment within Europe so that this escape route would no longer be available, persistent relative inflationary pressures in one part of the monetary union would tend to be punished by falling economic activity and rising unemployment'.

There are several reasons advanced for the need to keep the right to devalue: the need to deal with the structural disparities in the level of unemployment in different EU states, the need to take account of different economic cycles (Britain's for example does not seem to coincide with those of the rest of Europe) and to deal with outside shocks that may affect states differentially. It is also argued that German monetary union shows the dangers of rushing into EMU too soon; and that Britain's (and others') unhappy experience of membership of the ERM, and its success on leaving it, demonstrates the case against linking exchange rates.

We do not believe, however, that the structural disparities in the levels of unemployment of member states (accounting for a significant part of the discrepancies in early 1995 between, for example, (West) Germany at 5%, UK at 9%, Italy at 11%, Spain at 20%) are an argument against EMU. Europe has lived with these disparities for many years during which exchange rates have been flexible, which is consistent with the view that exchange rate adjustments do not affect levels of structural unemployment. The disparities are embedded in the economic, social and political development of — and often within — member states, and relate to different phases of modernisation and liberalisation (as well as to statistical variances). Structural unemployment is aggravated by imperfections in the labour market. They will take time to disappear, as economic reform and industrial investment and innovation transform the performance of the poorer member states. Structural unemployment is essentially a problem to be solved by the individual member state and is in itself no bar to membership of the EMU if other factors are convergent and the political will is robust.

What causes us more concern, in relation to the case for EMU, is unemployment caused by cyclical factors, or differential shocks affecting individual states. Oil price shocks and the case of German unification are often cited as examples. What is sacrificed in the pooling of sovereignty represented by EMU is the ability to respond to idiosyncratic events in one member state by changing exchange rates.

In fact it is very doubtful whether, in the closely integrated economies of Western Europe, outside shocks will affect member states differentially. They are much more likely to have a specific effect on particular industries or particular regions. Perhaps the true test of real convergence is the ability of regional economies to recover without persistent unemployment.

As for the different timing of the economic cycle, this is likely to be a temporary feature confined to the early stages of EMU.

There is a strong argument, therefore, for introducing a contra-cyclical financing mechanism in the operation of Stage Three until member states begin to perform to the same economic cycle. This would be of special benefit to the UK whose cycle is for historic reasons out of kilter with that of her major trading partners. Use of such a fund would have an overall neutral affect on the budgetary position of the Union over the medium term, as it would replenish itself according to the economic cycles. The real issue, however, is whether devaluation is an effective instrument and whether it could help to solve the problems of unemployment.

The limits of devaluation

States have used the right to devalue their sovereign currencies for a variety of reasons, ranging from wishful thinking to desperation. Whatever the circumstances, however, experience shows that the advantages of devaluation are all short-lived — econometric evidence suggests a half life of between three and four years. While immediate competitive advantage boosts exports, falling currencies seldom mean lower interest rates in the longer term — indeed, rather the opposite, which means that borrowing becomes more expensive and long-term investment more difficult. After decades of living with a currency of falling international value, the British public know very well that the 'pound in the pocket' does not retain its purchasing power. By way of compensation, falling currencies lead to higher wage demands. Where salary increases outstrip the growth of productivity, we have inflation. Inflation further reduces the value of money. If this process continues, the all-too-familiar pattern of economic decline sets in.

In TABLE TWO we show how sterling has declined in value against the Deutschmark over the past thirty years: the British pound is now worth one fifth of its value in 1965, and still falling. The evidence suggests that, given our high level of trade interdependence with the EU, devaluation is not an effective way to adjust, save in circumstances such as the bottom of the recession in 1992.

The 1992 experience was exceptional for several reasons. First, the UK recovery from economic stagnation had actually begun before the currency crisis. Second, the recession had been so bad and unemployment so high that there was enough slack in the British economy to absorb the shock of devaluation both in terms of a surge in exports and a rise in domestic demand. Third, although UK exports soared, so did world trade, which, in 1994 at 9%, showed the fastest growth for twenty years. For this reason, the French were able to resist the strong temptation to follow the British in a competitive devaluation and chose to stick with their *franc fort* policy: France, in other words, preferred parity with Germany, despite adverse social consequences in terms of unemployment, to parity with Britain.

TABLE TWO

Domestic and external value of the pound

Source: Financial Times

The decision in the UK about whether or not to join EMU will be based in part — and despite the post-1992 experience — on our long-standing apparent inability to use depreciation effectively. Will participation in Stage Three of EMU be the best way of reforming our economic performance? Could the Bank of England and the Treasury pursue price stability in a systematic manner without joining Stage Three? Alternatively, would the financial markets have the same confidence in an independent British monetary policy as they would in the monetary policy of the ECB and Ecofin? We return to these questions in the final section.

The experience of the Exchange Rate Mechanism

It has been argued by opponents of wider monetary union that repeated currency crises since the signing of the Treaty have obviated the case for EMU according to the terms and conditions of Maastricht. It is true that these crises have exposed the weaknesses in the Exchange Rate Mechanism. But Stage Three is crucially different to the ERM because it removes all uncertainty regarding exchange rates between the member states. It eliminates at a stroke all destabilising currency speculation within the single market — or at least in those parts of the market that are able and willing to participate.

In other words, there is a world of difference between a European Monetary System based on a grid of semi-fixed exchange rates (the ERM) and the single currency in an EMU. The former invites speculation — especially as the nominal exchange rates in the ERM got frozen after 1987 as people started erroneously to consider the system as a precursor to real monetary union. As the President of the European Monetary Institute, Alexandre Lamfalussy, has observed, for a whole series of reasons, good and bad, it was not possible to make the ERM function for long enough as planned, namely as a fixed but adjustable system of exchange rates.[28]

The British debate has been distorted by our bad experience of the ERM. It should not be forgotten, however, that the UK decision in October 1990 to join the ERM could hardly have been taken at a worse time. Sterling entered the ERM without negotiation when it was probably 10% overvalued and the DM was 10% undervalued. Recessionary pressures started to build up soon after the UK joined but the British labour market did not respond. The costs of overvaluation became increasingly clear and profit margins were squeezed, particularly in the export sector, leading to a substantial rise in unemployment. The National Institute of Economic and Social Research has concluded that at any time in 1990 or earlier, it would have been possible to announce the date of British entry to the ERM in advance, while at the same time announcing a significant reduction in interest rates.[29] The effect would have been to depress the entry rate of exchange substantially. Such a policy could even have achieved some of the benefits of Black Wednesday, when sterling was forced out of the system two years later, without incurring its costs.

Lessons from German unification

One of the factors which disturbed the smooth implementation of Maastricht and has since been cited as a warning against premature EMU was the severe shock dealt to the German economy and the rest of the European economic and financial system by the unification of Germany. This led to a policy of budgetary expansion balanced by monetary restriction which forced up Germany's short-term interest rates.

But the lessons of German unification for EMU are severely limited. The disparities between the two Germanies were huge, infinitely greater than the divergences between any of the candidates for EMU membership. In the German case, fiscal transfers eastwards amounted to 4% of GDP because German unification was a unique case of monetary union between two wholly disparate economies without any time to seek convergence, and at an exchange rate ludicrously out of line with unit labour costs. The 'shocks' that could be expected within EMU are unlikely to be in this order of magnitude, even if the Union were to prove to be unable to keep member states' deficits within 3% of GDP. In EMU we could be in a world where exchange rates are over-valued by an absolute maximum of 20%; not one in which they are over-valued, like the Ostmark (according to the black-market), by 400%.

Further, despite the enormous differences in productivity between East and West Germany, there were always bound to be irresistible pressures towards harmonisation of wage rates. Germany, after all, became one country. The force of the argument for wage equalisation between East and West Berlin, for example, was clearly very different from that affecting wage rates in the separate member states of the EU. There is no reason to suppose that a measure of wage differentiation to compensate for different rates of productivity cannot be maintained within EMU, as it has so far within the single market.

The ECB and the Bundesbank

The ECB is modelled formally on the German Bundesbank. Critics have argued that the comparative disregard by the Bundesbank of the social implications of their tight monetary policy would be perpetuated by the European Central Bank under EMU. Under the terms of the Maastricht Treaty, and as a guarantee against political interference that could undermine price stability, the members of the Governing Council of the ECB will not be allowed to take instructions from any other bodies. The Governing Council is to comprise the governors of the fifteen national central banks, and the members of the Executive Board which is to have a President, Vice-President and four other members appointed for an eight-year term. Although it must not be controlled by any political authority, there is scope for reinforcing the Bank's democratic accountability, and we return to this issue below.

It is a mistake, however, to think of the Bundesbank as a monetarist *deus ex machina*: in fact, it successfully combines independence with accountability. Above all the Bundesbank is a federal institution, rooted in the strong culture of German provincial banks, all of which have close relations with both sides of industry, the professions and the political parties.[30] The development of the EMU depends on how representative and federal the Union itself becomes — in other words, how power is decentralised within the European System of Central Banks and how articulate regional and industrial interests become in the European dimension.

Subject to the question of accountability, to which we turn next, the benefits of an economic framework of price stability in the European Union could be very substantial, particularly for countries such as the UK which have been bedevilled in the post-war period by stop-go policies that have exaggerated rather than smoothed cyclical fluctuations. Hans Tietmeyer, the President of the Bundesbank, has repeatedly emphasised that he expects the ECB to be able to perform the same crucial role of underpinning price stability upon which the German social market economy has been based. 'Anglo-Saxons', says Tietmeyer 'expect volatility in financial markets and for the central bank actively to manage interest rates by responding to every up and down of the business cycle: they still do not understand what the Bundesbank is up to'.[31]

Questions of accountability

It is axiomatic that the imposition of a single currency needs to command a popular consensus, and the new monetary institutions need to acquire quickly a high public reputation. The Treaty of Maastricht was disappointing in this regard. Although the EMU parts of the Treaty are by far the largest, most detailed and best prepared, they suffer from being unclear to all but a specialist readership. Moreover, the lines of democratic accountability are weak. In the third *Federal Trust Paper* we will be recommending institutional reforms to make the Union both more efficient and democratic. The Bundesbank President has emphasised repeatedly the need for a strong and democratic political framework to secure a context of political legitimacy and sound general policy within which an independent central bank can perform its function of ensuring currency stability. Here, however, we focus only on those aspects most directly touching the management of EMU.

The important Governing Council of the ESCB, which will meet monthly, is made up of the fifteen governors of the national central banks and the six independent governors of the ECB. The national bank governors will remain accountable to their respective national parliaments. For important decisions of the Governing Council, votes shall be weighted according to the national central banks' share in the subscribed capital of the ECB, and decisions shall be adopted by a qualified majority representing at least two-thirds of the capital and half of the shareholders. (A 'shareholder' is every member state having made the transition to Stage Three.) The six executive board members of the ECB are to be appointed for a non-renewable term by the European Council after having consulted the Governing Council of the ECB and the European Parliament.[32] The bankers will make an annual report to the European Council, Ecofin, the Commission and Parliament, including published accounts. The ECB shall be under the jurisdiction of the European Court of Justice, and enjoys, with the other EU institutions, the status of privileged litigant. The assent of the European Parliament is required if the statutes of the ESCB are to be changed; more significant changes need a Treaty amendment via the ordinary (and tricky) processes.[33]

The ECB will, of course, meet in secret and, unlike Ecofin, will not be expected to leak half-truths to representatives of the media. The President and members of the Bank and, indeed, of Ecofin may under present rules appear before the European Parliament, but we believe that more transparency and parliamentary scrutiny are desirable in the three areas of economic guidelines, multilateral surveillance and excessive deficit procedures.

At present, under the terms of Maastricht, Ecofin can act by qualified majority without consulting the Parliament. The European Parliament, however, has direct representative responsibilities too and it should be allowed to play a part in establishing the crucial democratic consensus over the direction of economic policy under EMU. We propose, therefore, that the

Parliament should at least be given consultative rights over the application of the excessive deficit procedure. The political effect of this reform would be that the economic and social objectives of the Treaty would be assured of receiving equal prominence with the monetary convergence criteria. We also propose that the appointment of the members of the executive board of the European Central Bank should require the assent of the European Parliament. This would be a stronger version of the procedure that currently pertains to the appointment of the Court of Auditors, where the Parliament is merely asked for its opinion on the relative merits of the candidates.[34]

'When the time is right'

One question raised by those who are not opposed in principle to EMU is: are we right to be pursuing it now? John Williamson has suggested that EMU in present conditions is too risky and should be delayed for 10 years.[35] Meanwhile he suggests a 'proto-EMU' with automatic exchange rate adjustments in response to different rates of price increases (a proposal somewhat similar to his earlier proposal of 'crawling-peg' exchange rate management). The merit of the Maastricht route is, however, that it avoids the half-measures of the past while it is itself sufficiently gradualist to give most member states a fair chance of adapting their economies to be ready for currency union without risking unacceptable hardship. The provision for derogations and the British and Danish opt-outs enable those member states that are not ready or willing to move to Stage Three to maintain a stable form of flexibility meanwhile. A mechanism such as Williamson suggests could serve them well during that stage. The idea of defining the 'normal fluctuation margins' required for the convergence criteria to include adherence to an agreed mechanism along these lines should indeed be seriously considered.

But there are strong political arguments against procrastination over the transition to Stage Three for those that fulfil the convergence criteria. It is a peculiar tactic to negotiate, sign and ratify a Treaty but then to cast doubt on its implementation. In contrast to British and Danish misgivings, however, at least a core of member states are likely to have the political will to adhere to the Maastricht timetable. The Treaty requires a core of states to go forward in 1999 and implies that that core should comprise a majority of the member states. Who forms the critical mass is not defined, but, again implicitly, it surely must include both France and Germany. The doctrine of unripe time, a well-known feature of the British debate about Europe, appears to hold out no solutions for Germany, France and their close partners.

In any case, as we have already noted, there will be some delay before EMU is complete.[36] The economic recession has made the transition to Stage Three before 1 January 1999 unlikely, in which case, the definitive decisions of the European Council will probably not be taken before early 1998. At that stage, the UK and Denmark might reverse their opt-outs, making it easier for Ireland and Finland respectively to take the plunge. Moreover, the rapid improvement to the Union's macroeconomic performance anticipated through 1996 and 1997 should transform the political atmosphere: the Commission is forecasting growth in GDP of 3.2% in 1996. Such growth should by then have enabled Austria, Belgium, Portugal and Spain (leaving only Greece and Italy aside) to have made good progress towards convergence, especially by cutting their all-important deficit/ GDP ratios.

Thereafter, practical difficulties concerning the production of new coinage and bank notes look certain to delay the actual introduction of the single currency. There will, therefore, be a few years when national currencies are locked together and the control of money supply has passed to the European Central Bank before we have full currency union and we begin to use Ecus as cash. (It is worth recalling that decimalisation in the UK enjoyed a five year transitional period.) The President of the EMI has told the European Parliament that the new bank notes will replace the old about three years after the beginning of Stage Three. The national mint directors have advised that a new currency could not be fully introduced for practical reasons until 2003: their incapacity to adapt to change will doubtless stimulate the introduction of electronic money kept in an 'electronic purse' for use in everyday shopping.[37]

There is a potential danger during this unavoidable transition period, however, that there could be heavy levels of conversion between currencies influenced largely by political factors. It will be important, therefore, to keep the interim period as short as possible, to promote the maximum use of the Ecu in inter-bank transactions, and to persist with policies conducive to economic convergence. To promote stability during the interregnum, there will at least be a single monetary policy dedicated to providing ECB guarantees in Ecus for any hard-pressed national currencies.

Certain specific decisions about the design of the new currency are also important. In our view, it might be preferable to keep certain national symbols such as the head of the monarch (or whomever) on one side of the new notes, but to have the obverse side of wholly common design. Our strong preference too, German sensibilities aside, is for the term 'Ecu', which is already quite commonly known, and to avoid decidedly any term with the prefix 'Euro'.

In real terms, however, these matters are comparatively insignificant: what matters to the citizen is savings in foreign exchange transactions and, above all, an end to the currency instability that affects investment and growth.

Should Britain take part?

We have examined above the criteria and timetable and implications for the Union of the transition to Stage Three. Our broad conclusion is that, despite some uncertainties, Economic and Monetary Union is both technically feasible and economically desirable and that, therefore, it could, should and probably will come to pass. The question now is should Britain take part? In the case of certain member states, for example Germany and the Netherlands, the economic case for a monetary union is very strong. It is less obviously so for Britain, but, on balance, our judgement is positive.

Opponents of integration argue that even if the federal core of member states of the Union form an optimal currency area, the UK is in a qualitatively different position because it is not so well integrated: it has different trading and foreign investment patterns, and it is subject to special influences, such as the dollar exchange rate and oil prices, which make it more at risk to asymmetric shocks. It was partly for these reasons that the government negotiated in the Treaty of Maastricht a right to 'opt-out' from participation in Stage Three.[38]

So the decision for Britain is not just difficult for political reasons. We have to be sure that it is in the British economic interest to pursue European integration — and we have to make up our minds quite fast. In fact, if the UK is to change its mind with regard to the 1999 date, it must say so by the end of 1997. If it does not, the UK will play only a peripheral role in the ECB, the ESCB and Ecofin. If and whenever the UK decides to participate it can do so without a Treaty revision: the 1996 IGC, then, need not be involved — although British credibility and influence in the IGC, and in the Union more generally, would be much strengthened by a political decision to proceed in a positive manner towards Stage Three of EMU. One thing is quite clear: hoping our partners will not go ahead without us will not stop them from doing so, and if they do the parameters of the British decision will be altered radically.

Retaining autonomy in monetary policy, however, is bound to have an appeal for any British government, not least because the 1992 devaluation appears to have been pulled off successfully. But as we noted above, the important issues are the interpretation of the convergence criteria, the manner in which Monetary Union is likely to operate, the quality of economic policies that are expected to flow from it, and the degree to which the British economy is already integrated with that of its European Union partners. It is in respect of these matters that Britain's choice on whether or not to participate should be taken.

There are two conflicting characteristics of the recent performance and behaviour of the British economy that bear on the effects of non-participation in EMU. The first is the fact that the supply-side of the British economy has become progressively more integrated with Europe. Examples are:

• joint ventures and other alliances between major British manufacturers and continental partners which follow an industrial logic attuned to the European market;

• the integration of financial markets in Europe and, increasingly, on a global level;

• the Europeanisation of key supply-side policies such as trade competition;

• and even the much vaunted success of the UK economy in attracting inward investment, for which the draw of European markets is plain.

Yet, curiously, there is a disjunction between Britain's economic cycles and those of our principal European partners, notably Germany. It can be argued that if this cyclical disjunction persists, the UK would be disadvantaged by policies set to reflect the circumstances of the broad mass of the European economy. This is why we have advocated a stronger contra-cyclical mechanism. Equally, it could be that the potential gains from supply-side integration are diminished *because* the UK's macroeconomy is out of step, and that enthusiastic participation in EMU would allow a more coherent path of economic development.

At present, the UK's competitive position is strong and EMU would help to lock us into that position and avoid the backsliding that habitually mars our domestic recoveries. Inside EMU Britain will be well-placed to take advantage of its relative labour market flexibility. The danger is that, if we stayed out, pay and prices would drift up again, and Britain would lose its competitiveness unless it devalued.

The principal advantages likely to be gained by Britain from membership of EMU are lower inflation and lower interest rates, with all the beneficial consequences that flow for investment and employment.

The evidence is overwhelming that Britain is likely to have lower inflation. No British government has been able to keep inflation as low as the rates achieved consistently over the years by the German Bundesbank: in fact, over the past 25 years our inflation has averaged 8.7%, more than twice that of Germany. The Governor of the Bank of England, no less, has supported the view that the European Central Bank is likely to run a better monetary policy than most national governments. With an independent ECB, British political parties will no longer be able to offer the electorate inflationary tax breaks; interest rates will not need to be hiked in order to save the pound; inflation will not be stoked by devaluation. The lower interest rates that would almost certainly follow from leaving monetary policy to an ECB closely modelled on the Bundesbank, and the end of the need to defend the pound, would not only help to increase investment but would be a very concrete benefit for all those struggling to pay off their mortgage. Lastly, as a member of the new European System of Central Banks, the Governor of the Bank of England will have more influence over German interest rates than he does now. The UK, which has paid a particularly high price for allowing partisan control of monetary supply and interest rates, stands to benefit highly from European monetary union. Lower interest rates would lead to more domestic investment and faster economic growth.

What happens if the UK stays out

The European Economic and Monetary Union will be weakened if Britain stays out. The addition of sterling to the weight of pooled national currencies would be most valuable in building the Ecu's role as an international reserve currency, with global contracts designated in Ecu, thereby removing uncertainty for European exporters. EMU plus the UK would contribute greatly to world financial stability — a goal which is jeopardised every day with the passage of $1 trillion across global markets.

That staying out of EMU would reduce Britain's influence in European policy-making is self-evident. Less obvious is what impact this would have. Switzerland, despite some apprehensions, does not obviously suffer from being surrounded by a European Union in which it has no formal voice. But Switzerland is small enough to be more or less politely ignored. Britain, as Europe's largest financial centre, is not, and would be seen as a major irritant and treated accordingly. In addition to political isolation, the UK would suffer all the main consequences of exclusion and marginalisation which, typically, affect peripheral regions. These include:

- a risk premium in the cost of capital;

- restricted access to relevant networks;

- lack of influence in the setting of rules and standards with damage to indigenous business interests;

- continued fuss and cost for British travellers on the continent;

- diminished attractiveness to foreign investors concerned to access the European market;

- obstacles for businesses seeking to sell to or invest in Europe, who will continue to face costs which their competitors no longer face.

In the debate about 'Britain in the world' it is often alleged that Europe matters less because everyone's future lies in securing a big share in the Pacific rim markets. Certainly these markets are proving profitable — for most — now. But they include highly unstable countries, and the risk is high. The fact that the UK trades in the Far East does not affect the case for EMU. In fact, a single currency would further diminish risk inside Europe, with greater potential for expansion there, and would certainly reinforce the UK's position in trade, development and, not least, political negotiations with the People's Republic of China. Further, Britain will be less well placed to compete in Asia if its industry is less competitive than its European rivals because it would face higher interest rates outside the EMU.

It is also claimed that US and Japanese multinational investors prefer our off-shore, low labour cost economy. The fact is that Germany as well as the UK attracts foreign investment, and the likelihood must be that foreign companies will be anxious to locate new factories inside not outside the new currency union.

If the single currency goes ahead without Britain, it is probable that the pound will continue to be subject to damaging speculation requiring the UK to keep a risk premium on interest rates of at least 1% over our competitors in the EU. The Bank of England has argued that London has always been an off-shore island, and that the City may become more competitive if UK banks remain free of continental non-interest bearing reserve requirements. But the City may lose business to its continental rivals as the Ecu emerges as a major world currency to rival the dollar and the yen: it will need to deal in and supply the Ecu market whatever happens, and to have to do so from outside EMU would surely put British banks at a competitive disadvantage.[39]

Safeguarding British interests

The United Kingdom economy is already on track to meet the Treaty criteria, despite fears about renewed inflation. However, in the state of present uncertainty about the UK's political disposition vis-à-vis Stage Three, it would be wise, in our view, for the government to take four steps to safeguard British interests:

- it should ensure that the UK meets the convergence criteria (a) because they make sound economic sense and (b) because it would keep options open;

- it should take steps to give the Bank of England greater independence of the Treasury in pursuit of price stability and exchange rate stability;

- it should continue to participate fully in the EU negotiations over the shape of Stage Three, the details of monetary policy and the conversion plans for the single currency;

- it should work hard to prepare the City of London for Stage Three.

The main point is that, whether we enter or not, the UK needs to continue to improve the competitiveness of its real economy in terms of unit labour costs, levels of structural unemployment, and, especially, productivity. This is the essence of the 'real economic convergence' which has been put forward as a condition for British entry into Stage Three. The UK economy is in fact at present competitive; and the more reform that takes place now, the more confident we can be that convergence will be sustainable in real terms.

The least difficult option in the circumstances would be to wait and see if the single currency is a success and then decide whether to join or not. But by that time the method of operation of the European Central Bank could have been decided without our participation. If the UK is not in the first wave of EMU it could be faced with a replay of other European policies, such as the CAP, which were drawn up to suit the original six member states. Those who forget history are condemned to repeat it.

Another option would be in effect to lease out the conduct of our monetary policy to the ESCB by locking sterling to the Ecu for a definite period. But this begs the questions, first, whether the contract would be accepted by our partners; second, whether it would be tested to destruction by the markets; and third, whether such a tentative approach would really instil the desirable long-term discipline.

On balance, and having weighed carefully the arguments, we are in no doubt that it is in the British national interest to participate in all aspects of EMU, including the single currency.

A decision to drop out of European economic and monetary integration would have serious political consequences. The move to EMU is the most important step taken by the European Union since it was founded. We should not underestimate the momentum now behind EMU and behind European integration generally. It is quite acceptable for states which share the common aim but are not yet ready for the single currency to postpone the transition to Stage Three until they have adapted their economies. But if Britain refuses to join even if we are qualified, we will be turning our back on the common purpose. It could be seen as a parting of the ways between ourselves and the rest of the Union. We could well face discrimination against us in the way directives were drafted or interpreted. Any devaluations by Britain outside EMU might well be regarded as unfair competition. Meetings of the Council in which Britain was out on a limb might become increasingly acrimonious; and in turn public opinion might become ever more hostile to the EU. It is not a fanciful fear that we 'might find ourselves in a one-way street leading out of the European Union'. [40]

The United Kingdom, therefore, should take the decision to join the single currency in principle as soon as practicable, and the government of the day should then promote the prospect of the new currency in the public domain for its positive advantages, lower costs and durable value. We are confident that such a strategy well-handled would come to command cross-party consensus and wide public support.

1 Several members of the Round Table contributed to this Paper under the guidance of Sir Roy Denman — in particular Dick Taverne QC.

2 Federal Trust Papers Number One, *State of the Union*, London, February 1995.

3 Article B.

4 Article 2.

5 EC *Bulletin*, Supplement 11/1970.

6 An altogether tougher approach was called for by a Federal Trust report by Giovanni Magnifico and John Williamson, *European Monetary Integration*, London, Federal Trust, 1972.

7 EC *Bulletin*, Supplement 1/1976.

8 For a full analysis of the EMU part of the Treaty, see Chapter V by Christopher Johnson in Andrew Duff, John Pinder and Roy Pryce (eds), *Maastricht and Beyond: Building the European Union*, London, Routledge for the Federal Trust, 1994.

9 Article 104c.11.

10 Notably, see Karl Lamers, *A German Agenda for the European Union*, London, Federal Trust and Konrad Adenauer Stiftung, 1994.

11 See Harry Cowie and John Pinder (eds), *A Recovery Strategy for Europe*, London, Federal Trust, 1993.

12 Churchill Memorial Lecture, Luxembourg, 21 February 1995.

13 Survey by MORI of Britain's 500 biggest companies, *Financial Times*, 13 February 1995. See also the CBI Survey, *The Single Market and the future development of the European Union*, November 1994.

14 *Opportunity or Threat: the single market reality for SMEs*, Pera International, 1993. According to Pera's survey, 70% of UK SMEs had experienced no business benefit from the single market.

15 Article 73b.

16 EC *Bulletin* Supplement 6/93.

17 See Dick Taverne (rapporteur), *The Pension Time Bomb in Europe*, London, Federal Trust, 1995.

18 For a fuller discussion of this phenomenon, see the Federal Trust Report, *Towards an Integrated European Capital Market*, London, Federal Trust, 1993.

19 We base these forecasts on Christopher Johnson, *Prospects for monetary union*, in 'European Trends', 1st quarter 1995, London, Economist Intelligence Unit, 1995. See also Christopher Taylor, *EMU: the state of play*, in 'The World Today', vol. 51, no. 4, April 1995.

20 Article 109j.1.

21 Article 104c.1.

22 Article 104c.2.

23 They are contained in Protocol No. 5 on *The excessive deficit procedure*.

24 Article 103.

25 COM (94) 333, *European Social Policy: a way forward for the Union*, European Commission, July 1994.

[26] The Edinburgh European Council in December 1992 agreed that the EC budget should rise to 1.27% of GDP by 1999; the Commission, backed by Spain, had proposed 1.32%.

[27] Churchill Lecture, op cit.

[28] Alexandre Lamfalussy, Statement to the Economic and Social Committee, 6 September 1994.

[29] Ray Barrell, Andrew Britton and Nigel Pain, *When the time was Right? The UK experience of the ERM*, paper presented to the ESRC conference on 'European Monetary Upheavals', 17 December 1993.

[30] By 'federal', we mean the dispersal of power between separate authorities according to the rule of law. It is a constitutional method of enabling liberal democratic states to live peaceably together and to manage their common affairs through a common government. See *State of the Union*, op cit, p. 29.

[31] Hans Tietmeyer interviewed by Will Hutton in *The Guardian*, 16 March 1995.

[32] See Protocol No. 3 of the Treaty on European Union on *The Statute of the European System of Central Banks and of the European Central Bank*.

[33] Article N.

[34] Article 188b.

[35] John Williamson, *Proto-EMU as an Alternative to Maastricht*, Paper presented at the European University Institute, Florence, July 1994.

[36] A view supported implicitly by the European Monetary Institute's *Annual Report 1994*, Frankfurt, April 1995.

[37] For a discussion of this phenomenon, see the forthcoming Federal Trust Report, *Network Europe and the Information Society*, London, Federal Trust, 1995.

[38] Protocol No. 11 on *Certain Provisions Relating to the United Kingdom of Great Britain and Northern Ireland*.

[39] This is the danger foreseen by the London Business School in its Final Report on *The Competitive Position of London's Financial Services*, London, March 1995.

[40] Paddy Ashdown, 'The case for a single currency', in *The Economist*, 4 March 1995. Even John Williamson, who would prefer a ten year delay in the whole enterprise, believes that if EMU does go ahead it would be better for the UK to be in than out.